Animals on the Farm

Cows

by Cari Meister

Bullfrog
Books

Ideas for Parents and Teachers

Bullfrog Books give children practice reading informational text at the earliest levels. Repetition, familiar words, and photos support early readers.

Before Reading

- Discuss the cover photo with the class. What does it tell them?
- Look at the picture glossary together. Read and discuss the words.

Read the Book

- "Walk" through the book and look at the photos. Let the child ask questions.
- Read the book to the child, or have him or her read independently.

After Reading

- Prompt the child to think more. Ask: Would you like to milk a cow?

Bullfrog Books are published by Jump!
5357 Penn Avenue South
Minneapolis, MN 55419
www.jumplibrary.com

Library of Congress Cataloging-in-Publication Data
Meister, Cari.
Cows / by Cari Meister.
   p. cm. -- (Bullfrog books: animals on the farm)
Includes index.
Summary: "A cow narrates this photo-illustrated book describing the body parts and behavior of cows on a farm. Includes picture glossary"--Provided by publisher.
ISBN 978-1-62031-001-4 (hardcover : alk. paper)
1. Cows--Juvenile literature. 2. Dairy cattle--Juvenile literature. I. Title.
SF197.5.M45 2013
636.2--dc23

                                    2012008222

Series Editor: Rebecca Glaser
Series Designer: Ellen Huber
Production: Chelsey Luther

Photo Credits: Alamy, 16-17, 23tl; Dreamstime, 3b, 4, 7, 10-11, 12, 13 (all), 20t, 20bl, 23 br, 24 20t; Getty, 5, 6, 9, 18-19, 19, 23ml, 23mr; iStockphoto, 22; Shutterstock, cover, 1, 3t, 8–9, 14, 14–15, 20, 21, 23bl, 23tr

Printed in the United States of America at Corporate Graphics in North Mankato, Minnesota
7-2012/ PO 1121
10 9 8 7 6 5 4 3 2 1

Table of Contents

Cows on the Farm

I am a cow.
I live on
a farm.

5

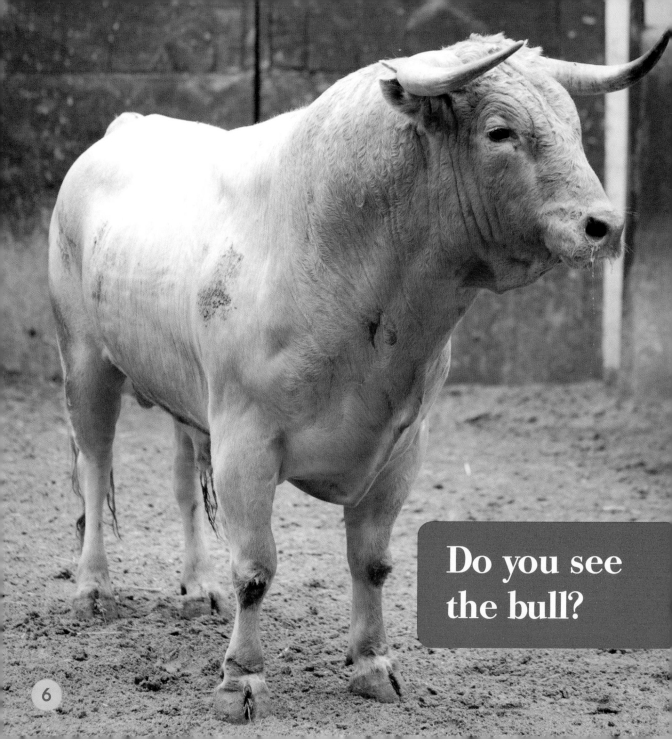

Do you see
the bull?

6

A bull has big horns.

calf ⋯▸

Do you see the calf?
She drinks milk.

Do you see the heifers?

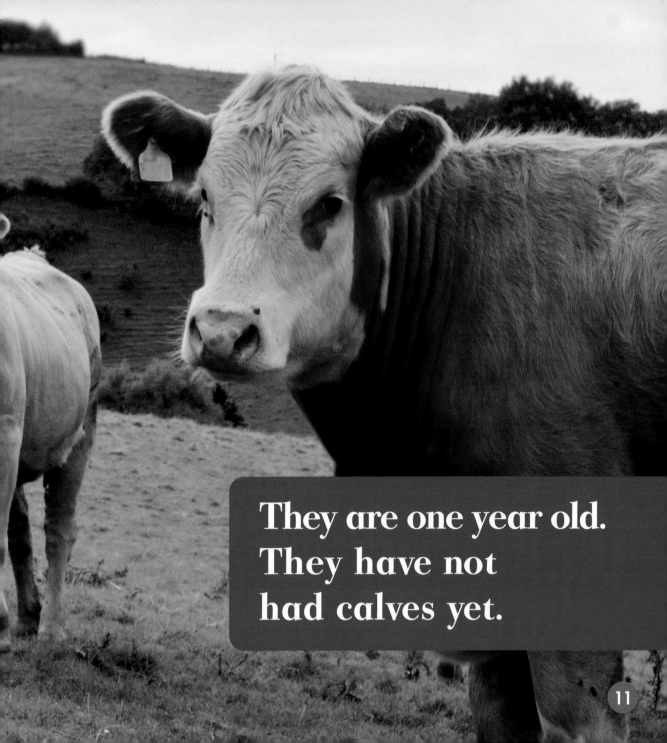

They are one year old.
They have not
had calves yet.

Do you see
my spots?
Spots are like
fingerprints.

All cows have
different spots.

Do you see me chewing?

I swallow my food.

It comes back up as cud.

I chew cud 8 hours a day!

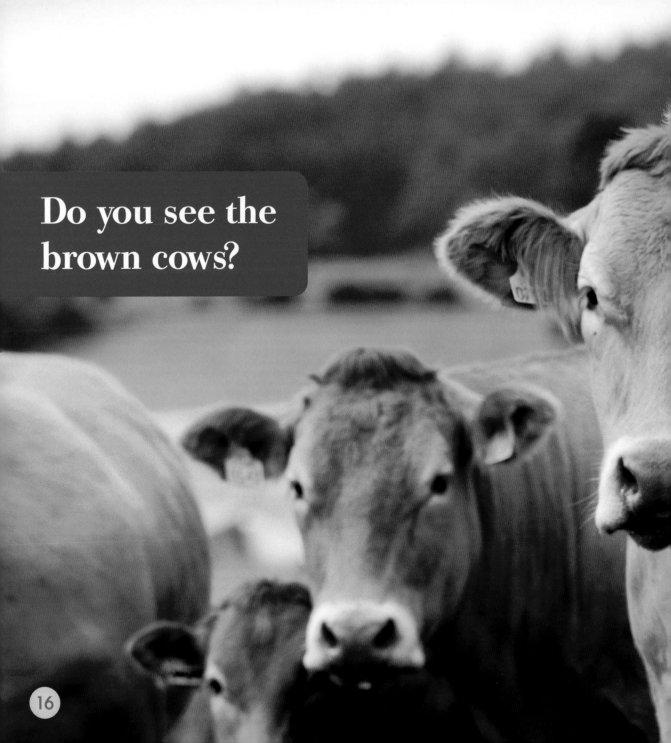

Do you see the brown cows?

They are beef cows.

Do you see the black and white cows?

They are
dairy cows.

They give milk.

Milk makes cheese.
Milk makes butter and yogurt.
It's a cow lunch!

Parts of a Cow

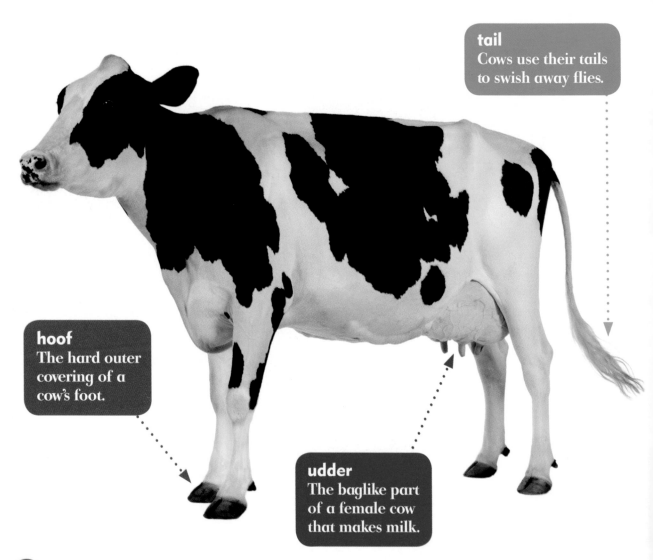

tail
Cows use their tails to swish away flies.

hoof
The hard outer covering of a cow's foot.

udder
The baglike part of a female cow that makes milk.

Picture Glossary

beef cows
Cows raised for meat.

cud
Food that comes back up from a cow's stomach and is chewed again.

bull
A male cow.

dairy cows
Cows raised for milk.

calf
A baby cow.

heifer
A female cow that has not yet had a calf.

Index

To Learn More

Learning more is as easy as 1, 2, 3.

1) Go to www.factsurfer.com

2) Enter "cow" into the search box.

3) Click the "Surf" button to see a list of websites.

With factsurfer.com, finding more information is just a click away.